13 Fashion Styles
Children Should Know

Simone Werle

PRESTEL

Munich · London · New York

Contents

What is fashion for? Surely not just to keep us warm. In earlier times the way you dressed was an indication of your social status and what kind of work you did. Later, after the Second World War, young people began to use clothing to express their views and their ideals. Today blogs and social networks make it possible for anyone to present her own look to the whole world with a simple mouse click or screen touch.

Throughout the twentieth century, fashion has constantly produced styles that were new, creative, and even revolutionary. The timelines in this book will help you fit these styles into their historical context. If you'd like to delve into the subject of fashion more deeply, you can follow the tips and suggestions and give the quiz questions a try. You'll find the answers at the back of the book, as well as explanations of terms that may be unfamiliar. These words are marked in the book with an asterisk (*).

Since we dress the way we feel, fashion is a reflection—in material form—of the times we live in.

Have a look yourself!

Madeleine Vionnet 1876–1975
Paul Poiret 1879–1944
Marchesa Luisa Casati 1881–1957

1882 electric street lighting in Berlin   1900 first subway line in Paris

1889 completion of Paris's Eiffel Tower

1880   1882   1884   1886   1888   1890   1892   1894   1896   1898   1900   19

Fashionistas*:
Marchesa Luisa
Casati, Irene Castle
Designers:
Jeanne Lanvin,
Madeleine Vionnet,
Paul Poiret
Make-up:
taboo!
Hairstyle:
loosely pinned-up
hairstyles
Accessories:
muffs, hats of every
kind, fans, parasols

The Century of Fashion Begins

Even at the very beginning of the twentieth century, there were already hints of where the fashion journey would lead. For the first time the motto was: do as you like!

Keep your smelling salts handy! At the beginning of the previous century women generally wanted to have an hourglass figure. This meant a full bust, a very small waist, and wide hips. To achieve their goal, women would be tightly laced into narrow corsets and their skirts adorned with wide "bustles."* But the tight corsets seriously constricted women's bodies, literally taking their breath away, with the result that they could sometimes faint or swoon. To revive them, strong-smelling substances—"smelling salts"—were held beneath the nose. It was time to for a change of thinking.

Fashion from France
Paris, 1912

Ready for a stroll?
Whenever a woman
left the house in sunny
weather, a hat and para-
sol were a must. Only
people who had to work
outdoors had tanned
skin: unthinkable for a
genteel lady!

1910 early movie producers established in Hollywood

1911 Coco Chanel opens her first fashion boutique in Paris
1912 the Titanic sinks in the North Atlantic
1914–1918 First World War

904   1906   1908   1910   1912   1914   1916   1918   1920   1922   1924   1926

**Emilie Flöge,
painted by
Gustav Klimt**
Vienna, 1902

This painting depicts
Emilie Flöge, who opened
the haute couture fashion
salon Schwestern Flöge
(Flöge Sisters) in Vienna
with her sister Helene.
The salon was decorated
in art nouveau style and
became a popular meet-
ing place for Vienna's
bohemian artist society.
The painter Gustav Klimt
designed a number of
dresses for Emilie Flöge,
none of which were
meant to be   worn with
a corset.

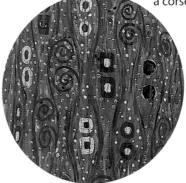

Tip
If you would like to see
more fashion from the
turn of the century, then
take a look at the art from
this period at your local
museum. There you can
discover many beautiful
patterns and clothing.

Wiener Werkstätte postcard
Vienna, c. 1911

The magnificently decorated, jungle-green hat creates a dramatic contrast with the narrowly cut ensemble and its large blocks of black and white. This outfit featured fabric called "Bergfalter" (mountain butterfly), which was designed by the artist Koloman Moser for the Wiener Werkstätte, a famous artist's workshop in Vienna.

Many social changes took place after 1900. Industrialization;* rising prosperity; a great interest in science, art, and philosophy; and the newly beginning women's movement* all had a great impact on fashion, which became more and more casual. Narrow lines and elegance, but also easier movement, were the most important features of the new woman's wardrobe. Some exceptions were the so-called hobble skirt, which had a narrow band below the knee that forced the wearer to take only tiny steps.

Favorite accessories included a fur-lined muff for keeping the hands warm in winter. A hat was absolutely required throughout the year. From 1910 onwards, hats became smaller and more outlandish. Small caps were decorated with large ribbons; veils and fabric flowers created an extravagant flair. Just like the clothing itself, the accessories, too, increasingly lost their classic function and form and instead became symbols of their wearer's taste.

Test yourself
What artistic movement or style does the large color illustration on the facing page belong to?
(Solution on page 46)

Activity
You can use silk flowers, bows, or ribbons to decorate a hat or cap yourself. They can be attached with a couple of loose stitches and taken off or redesigned whenever you want.

Gaby Deslys
France, 1910

Several accessories complement the softly falling dress worn by this French actress. A small clutch handbag, several strands of pearls, and a towering hat decorated with feathers complete the glamorous look.

Magician, pianist, and lady in eveningwear
Georges Barbier,
France, 1923

Many of the most important trends of the twenties can be seen here: chin-length hair, cherry-red lips, low-cut dresses, and ornamental jewelry for the head and hips. And something else is also striking: at the piano, quite naturally, sits a self-confident woman!

1922 G. BARBIER

Josephine Baker 1906–1975
Louise Brooks 1906–1985

1923 first issue of *Time* magazine
1927 first non-stop transatlantic flight
1928 discovery of penicillin
1929 stock market crash in the United States
1929 broadcasting of first television images

1916 1918 1920 1922 1924 1926 1928 1930 1932 1934 1936

The City Girls Arrive: Fashion in the Twenties

The Roaring Twenties: never have people had more zest for life than after the First World War. This vitality can be seen in their clothing.

Whether they were rich or poor, whether it was morning or evening, in the 1920s everyone suddenly began to wear the same thing all the time. This was unprecedented. And it happened because everyone once again felt like living, celebrating, and having fun together. The First World War was over and with it hard times were over, too. All of a sudden women were doing things only men had done: driving cars, going to work in offices, and enjoying sports. Even though this sounds completely normal today, at the time it was brand new. But to do all of these things, women needed new clothing.

Fashionistas*:
Louise Brooks, Josephine Baker, Suzanne Lenglen
Designer:
Gabrielle "Coco" Chanel
Make-up:
lightly powdered complexion, lips painted deep red (painted to make them look less wide, but fuller), eyebrows plucked thin, smoky eyes*
Must-have:
knee-length sack dress
Hairstyle:
chin-length bob, often with straight bangs
Accessories:
long strings of pearls, feather boas,* rolled-down stockings, cigarette holders, turbans,* feather headbands

Fun at the beach
USA, 1925

In the twenties, women bared their skin for the first time when they went swimming.

Did you know?
In the twenties
make-up was not only
for faces. In place
of transparent silk
stockings, ladies
simply powdered their
newly bared knees!

So, away with the tight corset, say goodbye to petticoats, off with the long braids. Otherwise how could she dance the Charleston? Women wore fancy turbans,* glittering headbands, knee-length skirts, and straight, chin-length hair. Their dresses were cut simply and hung loosely on their bodies to the knee. The cut of an evening dress was not much different from a dress worn during the day. Only the evening dresses tended to be lower cut (both in the front and the back) and more ornately decorated, with gold stitching, silk appliqués,* glass beads, and sparkling sequins. Accessories that went along with these dresses might include several strands of pearls or a long feather boa,* a delicate fan, and a small tulle* handbag.

And something else was new: all of a sudden it was acceptable to wear make-up. Lightly powdered skin, a dark-red, cherry-shaped mouth, and smoky eyes* below thin eyebrows were the first make-up trends of the twentieth century.

Simple elegance
London, 1920s

A popular look of the time was combining several, sometimes overly long strands of pearls with a day dress or evening wear.

Great evening attire
1925

Just because the silhouettes* were looser in the twenties did not mean they were lacking in extravagance.* Precious appliqués* of rhinestone and beads, a richly decorated train, elaborate head ornaments, and over-sized feather fans transformed their wearer into the queen of the night.

Tip
You can see more fashions of the twenties in silent movies from that era.

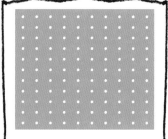

Fashionistas*:
Joan Crawford, Marlene Dietrich, Greta Garbo, Jean Harlow

Designers:
Elsa Schiaparelli, Cristóbal Balenciaga

Make-up:
velvety face powder, eye shadow (transparent during the day, colored at night), high eyebrows that were sometimes painted on, false eyelashes, red pouting mouth

Must-haves:
Bolero jacket,* princess-line dress,* Marlene Dietrich trousers*

Accessory:
belt worn at the waist

Hollywood stars of the thirties

Hollywood stars were the great fashion idols of the thirties. What they wore soon found its way into the closets and dressers of all women, usually in a simplified form. Especially popular: dresses that emphasized the waist.

A Wardrobe Crisis: Fashion in the Thirties

Fashion during the 1930s is unimaginable without the combination of blouse and skirt, which, along with the ladies' suit, became a favorite woman's look.

The world had quickly gotten used to the good life of the roaring twenties, but the fun was over just as soon. Money lost its value, factories and offices closed, and the overall mood got worse and worse. It's no surprise that people needed dreams of something better—or at least something nice to wear. In the thirties women looked towards Hollywood for inspiration. Dresses and hair became long and feminine again. During the day women wore suits—jackets and skirts—with narrow, button-down blouses. Shoulder pads created a wide and angular look, while the skirts fell softly to the calf in a bell shape. The only eye-catcher was generally a chic belt worn around the waist. The most popular dress of the thirties was the princess-line dress. Just like the fashions worn during the day-

1931–1971 the Empire State Building is
the highest building in the world

1933 Adolf Hitler becomes German chancellor

1938 during Kristalnacht,
Jewish businesses are
destroyed in Nazi Germany

1939–1945 Second World War

24   1926   1928   1930   1932   1934   1936   1938   1940   1942   1944   1946

**Woman wearing a dress
by the fashion designer
Mainbocher**
USA, 1930s

Princess-line dresses are
cut close to the body at
the waist. From the waist
down, the fabric falls
loosely along the body.
Such dresses were often
combined with a fur-lined
stole around the neck.

time, it was narrow and cut close to the body. But it had a lower neckline
that was often richly decorated with accessories. Add a pair of false eyelashes, velvety face powder, and carefully painted lips, and suddenly it was
possible to forget the hard times for a couple of hours.

Test yourself
After which real-life
princess was the princess-
line dress named?
(Solution on page 46)

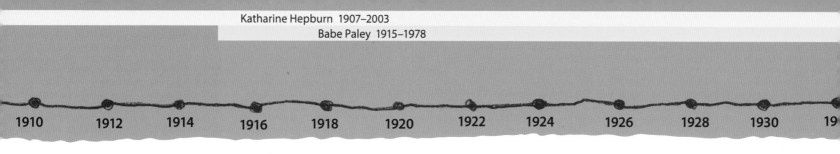
Actress
Barbara Stanwyck
USA, c. 1945

During the Second World War boxy suits in military colors were especially popular. Here the boxy shoulders, simple checkered pattern, and short tie were combined with a wide leather belt to emphasize the masculine look. Not much could intimidate someone wearing a suit like this!

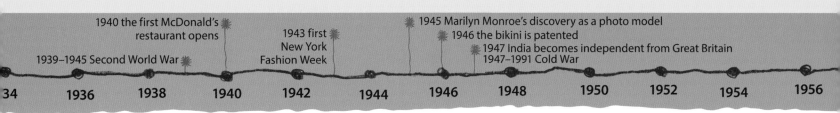

1940 the first McDonald's restaurant opens
1943 first New York Fashion Week
1945 Marilyn Monroe's discovery as a photo model
1946 the bikini is patented
1947 India becomes independent from Great Britain
1947–1991 Cold War
1939–1945 Second World War

34 | 1936 | 1938 | 1940 | 1942 | 1944 | 1946 | 1948 | 1950 | 1952 | 1954 | 1956

Everything Becomes Scarce: Fashion in the Forties

Practical clothing and austere colors: during the Second World War there was not much place for smart fashion.

During the Second World War it wasn't possible to walk into a store and simply buy what you wanted. Groceries, gasoline, and even clothing were rationed. This meant that even people who could afford it could not buy many new things. Just about everything was needed for the war effort. Almost every country issued its own clothing ordinances, which regulated every detail down to the maximum width of sleeves or belts and the length and number of pleats in a skirt. Expensive furs, decorative stitching, and other adornments were considered wasteful and absolutely taboo.

Throughout the world, but especially in war-torn Europe, women began to improvise. If they weren't allowed to purchase fashions then they would sew new clothing themselves from older pieces. But the practical purpose of this clothing was far more important than new trends or a beautiful appearance—after all, there were much bigger

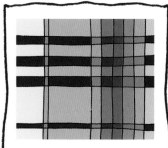

Fashionistas*:
 Babe Paley,
 Katharine Hepburn
Make-up:
 natural-looking eyes,
 shaped eyebrows,
 red lipstick
 (if available)
Hairstyle:
 ears free, rolled-back
 bangs, back and top
 layer in longer rolled
 curls

Fashion photograph
1944

Decorations like the pretty bow along the side of the hat here were an absolute luxury during wartime, and they were more likely to be worn by American women, if at all.

English everyday dress
Great Britain, 1943

Three photo models present the everyday wear collection of the British company Berketrex. To save fabric, the dresses and suits ended just below the knee and their cut is reminiscent of a nurse's uniform.

On the go in style
London, 1940

Seven photo models present new suits and coats in London. But although they're being modeled in Great Britain, the relatively chic wartime fashion was intended for the wealthier American market.

problems at the time than the way one looked. Various fabric remnants or old military coats were sewn into undecorated, simple suits or trousers. To save material, dresses went to just below the knee and were free of pleats and cut close to the body. Even shoes were reused so many times that they sometimes didn't fit quite right. But the fashion press made a virtue of necessity and simply declared this look to be a new trend—after all, there wasn't much of choice.

Trying on shoes
1943

Shoes with platform soles of cork and wood made it possible for women to stand above it all. And the best thing was that both of these materials were readily available, even in wartime.

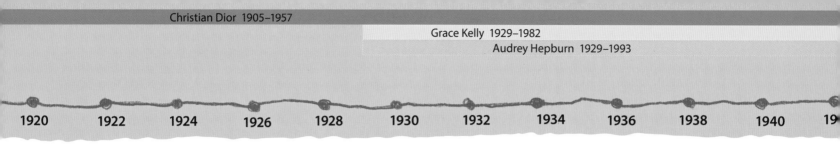

Fashionistas*:
Grace Kelly, Marilyn Monroe, Doris Day, Audrey Hepburn

Designers:
Christian Dior, Hubert de Givenchy

Make-up:
liquid eyeliner, no eye shadow, subtle rouge

Must-haves:
cardigan and petticoat

Accessories:
hat, gloves, handbag, and high heel pumps—all matching

A New Look: Fashion in the Fifties

During the fifties, one thing in particular was expected of women: they had to look beautiful.

To be precise, the fashion of the 1950s had already begun in 1947. This was the year in which a completely new look was presented in war-torn Paris. And what a look! Wide skirts, narrow waists, accentuated hips. Precious materials like satin,* taffeta,* and velvet* were used, all in wasteful abundance. No wonder the public's collective jaw dropped!

Fashion by Dior
France, 1951

The two most popular types of skirt during the fifties were the pencil skirt (in black) and the full skirt (in white).

During the war years women had to work very hard and do without many things. Now that the war was over they returned home, once again devoting themselves solely to their husbands and children. The war effort was over—but so too was their newly found independence. This can be seen in the fashion of the time. Feminine silhouettes,* floral prints, and an abundance of decoration such as flounces,* ruffles, and bows created a soft, but also inflexible, image of womanhood.

18

954 the first commercial nuclear power plant begins operation in Moscow ✳

1956–1959 construction of the Guggenheim Museum in New York ✳

1953 structure of DNA is identified ✳

✳ 1959 the first Barbie doll is introduced
at the New York Toy Fair

44   1946   1948   1950   1952   1954   1956   1958   1960   1962   1964   1966

Audrey Hepburn
c. 1955

Yellow and orange
blossoms on a pale
yellow ground: the dress
worn here by the famous
actress embodies spring-
time! Its flattering cut
features a small waist,
flared full skirt, decorative
ribbon, and girlishly short
sleeves. The accessories
are perfectly matched:
from the sunhat deco-
rated with flowers to the
quarter-length gloves.

Tip
You can see many
creations by fashion
designer Givenchy in
the Audrey Hepburn
films of the fifties.

Grace Kelly
Hollywood, 1955

People adored evening wear in the fifties, and they took it very seriously. There were strict distinctions drawn between cocktail dresses for the early evening, dresses for dinner and the theater, and the formal evening dress. The evening outfit was the queen of all dresses, worn only to great balls and official events.

Activity
With liquid eyeliner and an arm resting on a firm surface, you can line your eyes in a fifties-style dynamic curve.

Alongside the wide skirts (also called petticoats), another new kind of skirt appeared: the pencil skirt, which had a very narrow cut and fell to the knee. Pants, if they were worn at all, were only in the form of Capris, which ended just above the ankles. These were combined with blouses, twin sets,* and thin, narrowly cut cardigans in pastel colors. Accessories, however, were still a must: hats, handbags, and the popular high heel pumps—all in matching colors. In the evening women could display more elegance and grace. Cocktail dresses were richly decorated and their luxurious effect was accentuated by striking jewelry and gloves that reached to the elbows.

Marylin Monroe
Hollywood, 1952

The shortest skirts in the fifties ended just below the knee, never above it. This cream-colored pencil dress worn by the Hollywood beauty is combined with a pastel blue bodice with sewn-on bow and a cream-colored, long-sleeved Bolero jacket.* The make-up here is also classic for the fifties look: shiny red lipstick and thick black eyeliner on the upper eyelid.

Test yourself
Why are Capri pants named after a small Mediterranean island?
(Solution on page 46)

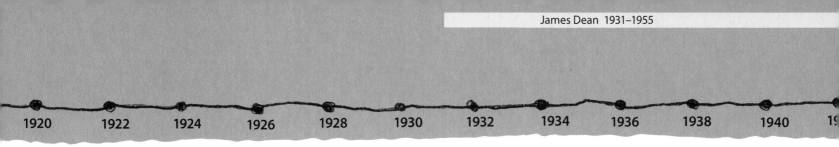

1920 1922 1924 1926 1928 1930 1932 1934 1936 1938 1940 19

Color:
  black
Make-up:
  thick black eyeliner
Must-haves:
  narrow trousers,
  narrow or very wide
  pullover sweaters,
  turtlenecks
Hairstyles:
  a simple ponytail
  or a neatly styled
  beehive*
Accessories:
  belt around the waist,
  beret,* very little
  jewelry

Black Replaces Pastels: The Cool Side of the Fifties

Not everyone agreed with the strict fashion requirements of the fifties.

And not everything in the fifties was light blue, soft yellow, or pale pink. The elegant but rigid post-war world also included a massive generation gap—a gap that was expressed in the fashions of daring young people.

The main color of the anti-look: black, black, and more black! In place of petticoat dresses, rebellious girls squeezed themselves into skintight black tops with or without turtlenecks and even tighter trousers. A wide belt completed the outfit. The only alternative for these girls: an oversized baggy pullover sweater with flat ballerinas or high-heel slip-on shoes. Italian sunglasses and the ever-fashionable beret* were the permissible accessories of the no-frills youth look. And the hairstyle? Carefully swept up but tousled, as if the wearer had just rolled out of bed.

Anita Ekberg
Sweden, 1951

A simple black t-shirt, three simple bracelets, and tousled hair: not much was required for the Swedish photo model's cool look.

Tip
The American rebel style can be seen in the films *Rebel without a Cause* with James Dean and *The Wild Ones* with Marlon Brando.

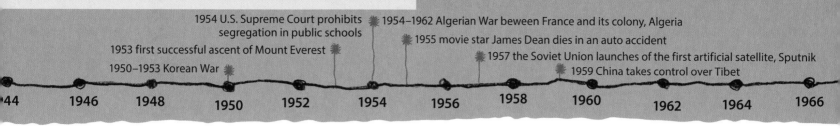

1954 U.S. Supreme Court prohibits segregation in public schools
1953 first successful ascent of Mount Everest
1950–1953 Korean War

1954–1962 Algerian War beween France and its colony, Algeria
1955 movie star James Dean dies in an auto accident
1957 the Soviet Union launches of the first artificial satellite, Sputnik
1959 China takes control over Tibet

44 1946 1948 1950 1952 1954 1956 1958 1960 1962 1964 1966

Josephine Douglas
London, 1957

A girl with rolled up jeans and a narrow, striped sweater strolls by two young men.

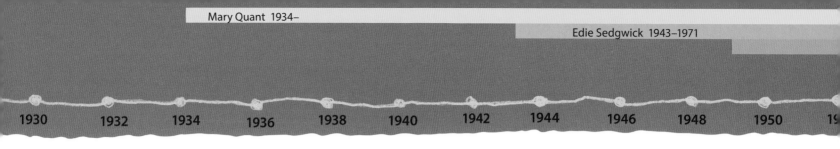
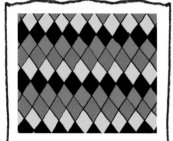

Fashionistas*:
Edie Sedgwick,
Twiggy
Designers:
Mary Quant,
Yves Saint Laurent,
Barbara Hulanicki
Make-up:
bright eye shadow,
black eyeliner, false
eyelashes on the
upper and lower
eyelid, bright lips
Must-haves:
miniskirts, boots,
vinyl* clothing
Hairstyles:
beehive* or smooth
and geometric
Accessory:
colorful plastic
jewelry

Chelsea-Girl
London, 1960s

Here we see the sixties
girl out and about with
a sleeveless turtleneck
mini-dress, white calf-
length vinyl* boots, and
a carefully backcombed
beehive* hairstyle.

Trends from the Street: Fashion in the Sixties

Clothing is now about the youth—and a short skirt
makes a big impact.

The times they are a-changin' ... If you were a teenager in the sixties, you
had a good chance to experience a wild life. The sixties were colorful,
loud, and, most of all, very youth-oriented.

For the first time in history, young people not only had their own ideas
but expressed them in their own style as well. And what a style it was: the
new short skirts made of
fabric and plastics, pants
in every shape and form,
and A-line dresses* in wild
patterns. Truly, these outfits had nothing in com-
mon with the serious adult
fashions of the fifties. And
that was the whole point,
for provocation was the
order of the day. Trends
no longer came from
designers but emerged
from the street.

Twiggy 1949–

1961 construction of the Berlin Wall ✹
1960 formation of the Beatles ✹

✹ 1962 premiere of the first James Bond film
✹ 1963 assassination of
U.S. President John F. Kennedy

1973 completion of the World ✹
Trade Center in New York City

954   1956   1958   1960   1962   1964   1966   1968   1970   1972   1974   1976

Twiggy
Great Britain, 1966

Lesley Hornby, known as "Twiggy," was the first world-famous super-model. Although she never saw herself as part of a movement, the extremely slim English woman with the innocent look rapidly became a fashion icon. Here she is wearing a pink A-line dress* and silver ball earrings with a straightened bob and false eyelashes.

Youthful elegance
1963

The sixties also had its conservative fashions. But they were much fresher than the looks of previous decades. The adult version of the youthful sixties look consisted of loosely cut coat dresses without waists, and straight cut sheath dresses made of stiff fabric with a matching coat. Popular accessories were clutch handbags, gloves, and the pillbox hat: a round, flat hat that sat on the back of the head.

The striking looks were topped off with wide plastic bracelets and over-sized earrings, which competed for the viewer's attention with garish eye shadow, thick eyeliner, and masses of false eyelashes. And there was one accessory that proved quite useful with the newly popular miniskirt: tights that covered up any problems "below." The short skirts made the wearer's legs look extra long; and lurex,* crocheted, and lace tights in every color—as well as fishnet stockings with elastic yarn—showed them off properly and added another splash of color to the outfit.

Stark contrasts
France, 1968

Clear lines, strong colors: people in the sixties were not into pastels. The models here are presenting the collection of French designer Andre Courreges. All are draped entirely in red and white.

Activity
You can make a sixties-style beehive* hair-do by backcombing your hair and using a generous amount of hairspray. Short geometric cuts look best with completely straight hair.

Test yourself
In which city did the miniskirt begin its triumphal march?
(Solution on page 46)

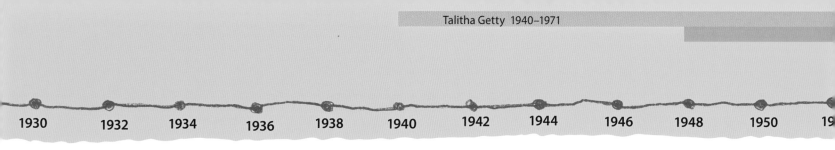

1930   1932   1934   1936   1938   1940   1942   1944   1946   1948   1950   19

Fashionistas*:
  Talitha Getty,
  Stevie Nicks
Make-up:
  completely natural,
  tanned complexion,
  painted flowers
Must-haves:
  peasant top, caftan,
  fur vest
Hairstyle:
  long, air-dried hair
  parted in the middle
Accessories:
  bells, round sun-
  glasses, ethnic
  jewelry,* headbands

Fabric and Love: The Fashion of the Hippies

From mini to maxi: in the second half of the sixties fashion became the expression of a new lifestyle.

There was one thing a true hippie wanted more than anything else: to be free. She wanted to be free of constraints, free from violence, and free to choose what she would wear. And of course no one wanted this freedom just to look like everyone else. So traditional suits for men or women were out; blouses and mass-produced uniforms were taboo. Instead, people wanted to wear individual, "authentic" clothing, inspired by the cultures of foreign lands like India, Morocco, or South America. It didn't matter where, as long as it was unconventional.

Hippies wore their hair long with a part in the center, and they had long wide skirts, flared jeans, exotic caftans, and sandals. The jingle of the little

Hippie girl
left, London, 1967;
right, Rome, 1970

Ethnic* pieces like lamb-skin vests and home-made batik blouses were popular among hippie girls. Such clothes gave them the natural look they desired.

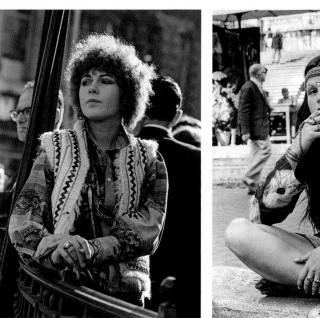

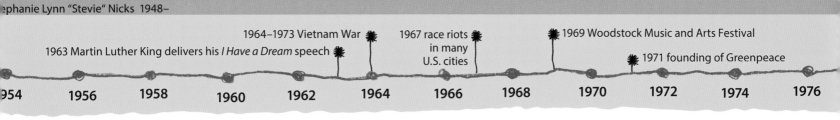

1964–1973 Vietnam War

1963 Martin Luther King delivers his *I Have a Dream* speech

1967 race riots in many U.S. cities

1969 Woodstock Music and Arts Festival

1971 founding of Greenpeace

954   1956   1958   1960   1962   1964   1966   1968   1970   1972   1974   1976

Hippie girl
Pittsburgh, 1967

Typical hippie: long open hair, a blouse embroidered with flowers, and flared blue jeans.

bells they used as accessories could be heard everywhere. These were paired with fur vests, strings of beads, colored scarves, and colorfully embroidered peasant tops. Embroidery covered everything. Hippie girls summoned up their artistic abilities and decorated their outfits with "flower power"* blossoms in colorful yarn.

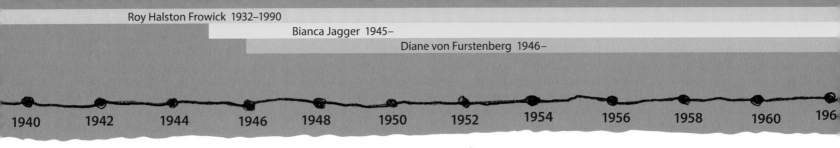

A summer stroll

1972

There was no fear of kitsch in the early seventies. The two romantic outfits are richly decorated with flower patterns. Blouson sleeves and platform shoes were typical of the times.

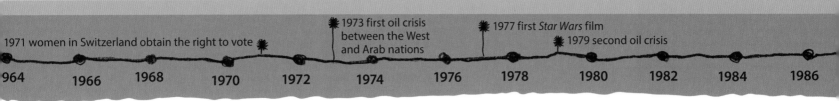

1971 women in Switzerland obtain the right to vote ✳   ✳ 1973 first oil crisis between the West and Arab nations   ✳ 1977 first *Star Wars* film   ✳ 1979 second oil crisis

964   1966   1968   1970   1972   1974   1976   1978   1980   1982   1984   1986

Colorful, Loud, and Free: Fashion in the Seventies

Bell-bottomed pants and garish colors created eye-catchers in the seventies closet.

Fashion in the seventies picked up where the hippies of the sixties left off. Only now, the free look of the hippies could be worn by everyone. Even though no new forms, cuts, or silhouettes* were created during this time, there was still plenty to look at.

Nothing could be too tight, too short, too wildly patterned, or even too colorful. And most of all nothing could be too exaggerated. Multicolored and decorated pieces of clothing were made of polyester fabrics, ultra high platform shoes, satin bomber jackets,* maxi coats with crazy appliqués,* and pants with bottoms that seemed to flare out endlessly: the wild seventies truly had no fear of kitsch. "Everything goes" was the motto, even when combining completely opposing styles. You could leave your house in the morning without make-up in an organic, Indian-inspired look; and just as easily hit the dance floor at night in a cowboy-inspired disco outfit with blue glitter liquid eye shadow.

Fashionistas*:
   Carolina Herrera, Bianca Jagger, Veruschka

Designers:
   Roy Halston Frowick, Diane von Furstenberg, Calvin Klein

Make-up:
   liquid eye shadow in blue, green, or silver; light opalescent lipstick; eyeliner and thickly mascaraed eyelashes

Hairstyle:
   natural-looking blow-dried waves

Accessory:
   platform shoes

Extravagant evening look, Madrid, 1970

A striking outfit: the strongly contrasting black-and-white print of the one-piece suit is repeated in the matching wrap. A black shawl flung around the head and large earrings round off the ensemble.

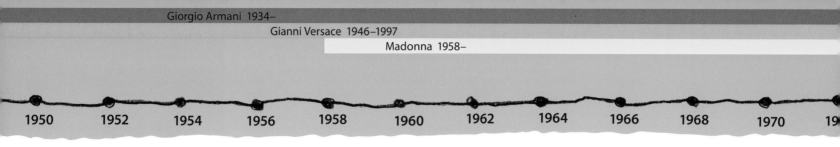

Fashionistas*:
Princess Gloria von Thurn und Taxis, Princess Diana, Madonna

Designers:
Giorgio Armani, Gianni Versace, Christian Lacroix

Make-up:
garish eye shadow, blue and green eye-liner and mascara, gaudily colored lip gloss

Must-haves:
designer clothing, shoulder pads, a walkman, leggings, stone-washed jeans

Hairstyles:
piled high, sprayed, and permed; the mullet (short in front, long in back)

Accessories:
Ray Ban sunglasses, neon-colored jewelry, leg warmers,* bags with logos

Cher, Los Angeles, 1984

This brightly colored clothing for aerobics makes exercising fun!

Show What You've Got: Fashion in the Eighties

Success, fitness, and consumerism shaped the mood of the decade.

The 1980s were a time of extremes. Romantic lace met coarse leather, tennis shoes met business suits, and neon-colored accessories met pastel-colored polo shirts and faded blue denim jeans and jackets.

Whereas earlier, people tended to show what they stood for, in the eighties people began to show what they had. Whoever could afford it made a bold display of her wealth with brand-name clothing and large logos. Short jackets and blouses with wide shoulder pads, tight skirts with narrow waistlines, bustiers, and hair that was permed, piled high, and sprayed created the striking contours of this self-confident power look.

Of course, a style this superficial also required the right figure. The cult of sports and aerobics helped people shape their bodies until there was nothing left to shape. With the help of skin-tight fabrics, the fitness-obsessed eighties girl left little to the imagination. Leggings, bicycle pants, and cropped sweatshirts were no longer just worn for sports. They also influenced fashion on the streets.

32

1981 first flight of the space shuttle ✳
1980–1988 First Gulf War ✳

1983 production of the first mobile telephone ✳
1986 Chernobyl nuclear disaster in what is now Ukraine ✳
1989 fall of the Berlin Wall ✳

74   1976   1978   1980   1982   1984   1986   1988   1990   1992   1994   1996

Madonna
New York, 1984

In the eighties, the singer Madonna was the first to combine a harsh punk look with girlish New Romantic elements. Here she wears a faded jeans jacket with graffiti-like drawings inside out, tousled hair, an abundance of costume jewelry, and striking purple make-up.

Tip
Music videos, which became popular in the eighties, are a good place to find the various looks of the time.

Alicia Silverstone in
Clueless

USA, 1995

Shop 'til you drop. In the trendy nineties film *Clueless*, the perfect look involved many fashion ideas mixed together. Here actress Alicia Silverstone wears a short, straight plaid skirt with knee socks, silver Mary Jane shoes, and a blazer: a combination typical of the times.

Wear What You Hear: Fashion in the Nineties

From grunge to techno: the nineties made music into fashion.

On the catwalks of the 1990s there was a simpler, toned-down approach. Minimalistic* forms, muted colors, and light-weight materials were the designers' response to the extravagance* of the eighties. But not everyone wanted this look. While the fashion press celebrated understatement,* the youth aligned themselves more with what came out of their loudspeakers. And just as there was not one kind of music, neither was there only one fashion trend in the nineties. Even within the boy groups and girl groups that were popular at the time, each member had his or her own look.

If you listened to hip hop, for example, you wore low-waisted pants; large, long t-shirts or tights; short tops; white down jackets; and as accessories heavy gold chains, baseball caps, and eye-catching athletic shoes.

Fans of techno music preferred colorfully dyed, plaited hair, loud colors, and clothing made of synthetic materials. Their outfits were marked by contrasts: wide, overly long pants were combined with tight, cropped shirts and shoes with extremely high platform soles. The party look was completed by bold face painting, flowers, whistles, and glowing armbands.

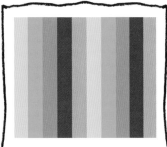

Fashionistas*:
Kate Moss, Gwen Stefani, Carolyn Bessette-Kennedy
Designers:
Jil Sander, Helmut Lang, Donna Karan, Stella McCartney
Make-up:
subtle nude look,* lipstick in dark colors or skin tones
Hairstyle:
two-tones: the hair on top a different color from the hair around the shoulder

Activity
You can take your fashion cue from your favorite music today.
Just have a look at the bands and singers you like best!

Kate Moss
New York, 1995

For this photo shoot the British supermodel Kate Moss is wearing a purple example of the minimalist* look.

Followers of "grunge" style on the other hand wanted most of all to look like they hadn't given a thought to what they wore. Plaid flannel shirts, faded jeans, wool caps, long stringy hair, and worn-out Converse All Star sneakers or Doc Martin boots created the desired look. This style even made it into fashion magazines in a "cleaned-up" version. Who would have guessed?

Two Harajuku girls
Tokyo, 2000

In Japan, girls who always have fashion on their minds are called "kogyaru." But not all Harajuku girls wear their completely crazy look every day— many save their best outfits for Sunday afternoons in Harakuja. These two girls are not followers of any one particular style, but mix different Harajuku elements into their own colorful look.

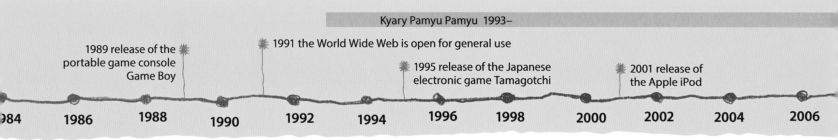

Kyary Pamyu Pamyu 1993–

1989 release of the
portable game console
Game Boy

1991 the World Wide Web is open for general use

1995 release of the Japanese
electronic game Tamagotchi

2001 release of
the Apple iPod

984 1986 1988 1990 1992 1994 1996 1998 2000 2002 2004 2006

The Crazy Look from Japan: Harajuku Style

The cute look of the cool girls in Tokyo conquers the world.

On Sunday afternoon there's a specific place where fashion-conscious girls (and boys!) in Tokyo gather: Harajuku. The area around Harajuku train station in the city district of Shibuya is not only a perfect place to go shopping, listen to music, and meet friends; it's also an enormous catwalk.

Fashionistas*:
  Minori, Kyary Pamyu Pamyu, Hirari Ikeda
Designer:
  Kumamiki
Make-up:
  eyes painted in a child-like style, complexion either pale or deeply tanned
Hairstyle:
  exaggeratedly childish look, often with bangs and all shades of colors
Accessories:
  cute barrettes, leg and wrist warmers,* bracelets, over-the-knee socks, bags, trinkets

Harajuku style

Here we see Japanese Lolita Girls on the Takeshita Dori street in Harajuku.

Harajuka Style is not one single look. But what all its different styles have in common is that they are "kawaii" (Japanese for "cute") and definitely not meant for the everyday. The Japanese youth describe their look as "cosplay," short for "costume play."

Especially popular is the Lolita Style, which mixes nineteenth-century Victorian fashions—such as petticoats and ruffled blouses—with colored leg warmers,* plenty of girlish accessories, and doll-like make-up. Ganguro Girls take their cue from the sunny look of California and push it to the limit. Deeply tanned skin, extremely light-colored eye-shadow, and white-blonde hair complement the bright colors of the clothing in orange, pink, red, yellow, and turquoise. The Gothic Girls on the other hand avoid color completely. Their somber look is either entirely black (Kuro Girls) or snow white (Shiro Girls).

If you're looking for inspiration for your own Harajuka Style, there are numerous Japanese magazines that deal with nothing other than Harajuku. These magazines give detailed styling tips and step-by-step instructions for the right make-up.

Did you know?
Fashion in Harajuku style is sold internationally on the internet. Useful search terms are Harajuku, Shibuya, and kawaii.

Tip:
More Harajuku street-style photos can be found on Japanese fashion websites like http://www.style-arena.jp, and http://tokyofashion.com/.

Harajuku Lolita Girl

Many elements of the Lolita look can be seen here: a Victorian-style blouse, a skirt cinched around the waist and worn with a petticoat, and a girlish hairstyle with an enormous lace bow. Japanese girls prefer to stand (and sit) with their toes pointed inwards—this is considered very "kawaii."

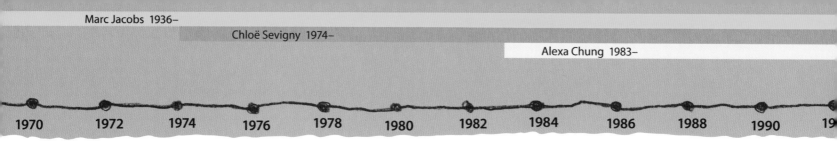

Fashionistas*:
Chloë Sevigny, Sienna Miller, Agyness Deyn, Alexa Chung

Designers:
John Galliano, Tom Ford, Marc Jacobs, Hedi Slimane, Alexander McQueen

Must-have:
fashion blog

Hairstyles:
loose bun on top of the head, braided styles

Accessories:
smart phone, nerd glasses, statement bag

Look What I'm Wearing: Fashion in the Early Twenty-First Century

Rapid trends and fashion blogs: in the new millennium anyone can become a fashion icon.

You might think that at the turn of the millennium a completely new look arose. But guess again. Since the beginning of the 2000s, fashion has been mainly concerned with looking back—at a whole century full of styles.

Earlier, young people often used their appearance to reveal what they felt or thought, or to show off their social status. In the twenty-first century, people mostly want to wear what they like. The fashion of the new millennium often quotes the most important trends of the past and creates individual looks from this rich store of style elements. Slim jeans,

Mixing patterns
Istanbul

The close-fitting one-piece suit in a tiger print is visually broken up by the short gray shirt and its bold eyeglasses motif.

42

2002 introduction of the euro ✸
2001 September 11 attacks in the US ✸

✸ 2003 the human genome is decoded
✸ 2004 founding of the online community Facebook
✸ 2007 first Berlin Fashion Week

94   1996   1998   2000   2002   2004   2006   2008   2010   2012   2014   2016

Totally relaxed
Istanbul

The short dress with "statement" print is complemented by loosely worn hair, colorful armbands, and boxy white glasses. A must: the smart phone, which can photograph the look and send it to others with the touch of a screen.

leggings, nerd glasses, or overalls: none of these are new, they're simply combined in new ways.

And since there are so many possibilities in the choice of clothes, everyone can think very carefully about how they actually want to look. The ones who do this thoroughly also want to be seen, of course: not only on the street but also around the world on the internet. With fashion blogs, street style portals, and social networks, anyone can potentially become an international fashion star—all he or she needs is a good look and a camera!

**Jools rides
a Pashley Princess Sovereign**
London

A black roadster bike is a
hip way of getting around,
especially in the city. The
pink flowers decorating
the basket match the floral
pattern of the close- fitting
shorts and the pastel color
of the sleeveless top.

Glossary

A-LINE DRESS is a dress with a straight cut that flares out towards the bottom

APPLIQUÉ is sewn-on decoration of fabric, leather, or felt

BERET, a round flat cap of wool felt

BEEHIVE is a teased hairstyle combed upwards and reminiscent of a beehive

BOLERO JACKET is a short, open jacket generally with long sleeves

BOMBER JACKET is a short, close-fitting jacket with knit cuffs

BUSTLE is a type of framework worn under the skirt to make the back of the dress look fuller

ETHNIC JEWELRY makes use of the indigenous styles of many cultures

EXTRAVAGANCE means being intentionally excessive in decoration or cost

FASHIONISTA is a fashion-conscious woman who sets new trends

FEATHER BOA is a decorative scarf made of feathers

FLOUNCE is a wide ruffled strip added to a piece of clothing

FLOWER POWER. The flower was a hippie symbol for a peaceful society

INDUSTRIALIZATION, a period in history when people began buying factory-made clothes and other goods instead of making them at home

LEG WARMERS / WRIST WARMERS, a kind of tube open on both ends, generally knit, to warm the legs or wrists

LUREX STOCKINGS are stockings with a shiny look

MARLENE DIETRICH TROUSERS are waist-high pants with a crease and wide legs, first made popular by German movie star Marlene Dietrich

MINIMALISM, in fashion, refers to outfits that avoid fancy, elaborate decoration

NUDE LOOK, a make-up style in which the wearer looks like she's not wearing make-up

SATIN is a smooth, shiny fabric

SILHOUETTE is the form made by the body's contours

SMOKEY EYES are darkly made-up eyes

TAFFETA is a crisp silk fabric

TULLE is a fine, net-like fabric

TURBAN is a scarf wraped around the head

TWIN SET, a generally short-sleeved sweater and cardigan of the same color and fabric

VELVET is a soft fabric with a downy surface

VINYL (PVC) is a type of plastic

WOMEN'S MOVEMENT is a movement that promotes equal rights and opportunities for women

UNDERSTATEMENT, something that has been made to look simple and unfussy

Answers to the questions:

page 7:   The colored illustration is an art nouveau (or Jugendstil) work.

page 13:   The princess-line dress was named for Princess Alexandra of Denmark, the wife of British King Edward VII.

page 21:   Sonja de Lennart, the inventor of Capri pants, liked to take her vacations on the island of Capri.

page 27:   The miniskirt began its worldwide victory march in London.

© Prestel Verlag, Munich · London · New York, 2013

Picture credits:
Cover images, frontispiece, p. 4, p. 6,
p. 7, p. 8, p. 9, p. 10, p. 11, p. 12, p. 13, p. 14, p. 15, p. 16,
p. 17, p. 18, p. 19, p. 20, p. 21, p. 22, p. 23, p. 24, p. 25,
p. 26, p. 27, p. 28, p. 29, p. 30, p. 31, p. 32, p. 33, p. 34,
p. 36/37, p. 38, p. 39, p. 41: Getty Images; p. 42, p. 43:
© Ivan Rodic; p. 44: © Horst Friedrich

Prestel, a member of Verlagsgruppe
Random House GmbH

Prestel Verlag, Munich

www.prestel.de

Prestel Publishing Ltd.
14-17 Wells Street
London W1T 3PD

Prestel Publishing
900 Broadway, Suite 603
New York, NY 10003

www.prestel.com

Library of Congress Control Number is available; British
Library Cataloguing-in-Publication Data: a catalogue
record for this book is available from the British Library;
Deutsche Nationalbibliothek holds a record of this
publication in the Deutsche Nationalbibliografie;
detailed bibliographical data can be found under:
http://dnb.ddb.de

Prestel books are available worldwide. Please contact
your nearest bookseller or one of the above addresses
for information concerning your local distributor.

Translated from the German by: Cynthia Hall
Copyedited by: Brad Finger
Design: Michael Schmölzl, MIUCHEI, München
Layout: Meike Sellier
Production: Astrid Wedemeyer
Lithography: ReproLine Mediateam, Munich
Printing and binding: Printer Trento, Trento

Verlagsgruppe Random House FSC® N001967
The FSC®-certified paper Profibulk has been
supplied by Igepa.

ISBN 978-3-7913-7134-4